CONTENTS

Facing page View from the quire towards the west end

Truro Cathedral Office
14 St Mary's Street, Truro, Cornwall TR1 2AF
Telephone: 01872 276782
Fax: 01872 277788
Email: info@trurocathedral.org.uk
www.trurocathedral.org.uk

INTRODUCTION

Truro Cathedral stands at the heart of Cornwall's main retail and administrative centre, the focal point of the city. A glorious building, its three magnificent spires soar heavenwards dominating the city's skyline. People are surprised that a building that looks like it harks back to the Gothic Middle Ages is in fact little more than 125 years old. The main foundation stone was laid by the Duke of Cornwall, and future Edward VII, on 20 May 1880. It was the first new cathedral to be built in this country for well over 600 years since Salisbury was begun in 1220. Today the Cathedral receives around 200,000 visitors a year; some attracted by prayer, worship or music;

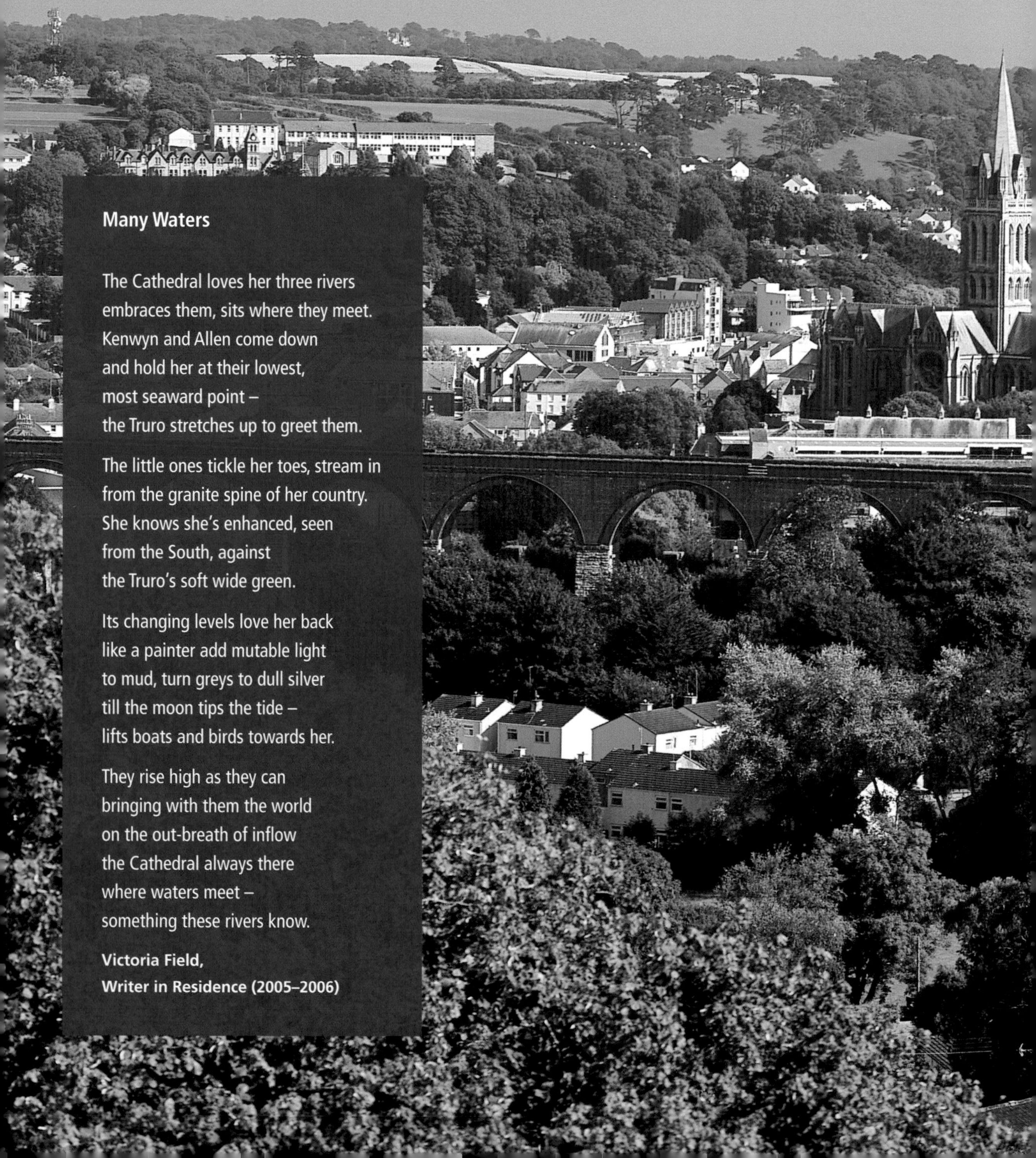

Many Waters

The Cathedral loves her three rivers
embraces them, sits where they meet.
Kenwyn and Allen come down
and hold her at their lowest,
most seaward point –
the Truro stretches up to greet them.

The little ones tickle her toes, stream in
from the granite spine of her country.
She knows she's enhanced, seen
from the South, against
the Truro's soft wide green.

Its changing levels love her back
like a painter add mutable light
to mud, turn greys to dull silver
till the moon tips the tide –
lifts boats and birds towards her.

They rise high as they can
bringing with them the world
on the out-breath of inflow
the Cathedral always there
where waters meet –
something these rivers know.

Victoria Field,
Writer in Residence (2005–2006)

some out of curiosity; and some just to escape the weather or hustle and bustle of the city! All are welcome, all embraced in the love of Christ.

This Souvenir Book seeks to capture a little of the essence of Truro Cathedral, through a mixture of words and images: as a place of worship, music and pilgrimage; an oasis of peace and centre of creativity; a focus of unity and centre of evangelism; a place of reconciliation and dialogue; an architectural wonder; and as the Mother Church of the diocese.

We hope it will be an inspirational reminder of the day you visited Cornwall's Cathedral in the Land of the Saints.

The background to the building of this modern cathedral has its origins in the time when Cornwall had its own bishop at St Germans, near Saltash, with its own Saxon cathedral. It appears that Viking raids forced the move of this original Cornish diocese, to be held jointly with the Devon diocese at Crediton, and then in 1050 at Exeter. Effectively the Cornish diocese, with its own bishop and cathedral, ceased to be a separate entity. For over 800 years the Cornish Church was administered from Exeter, but in 1877, after 30 years of very intense lobbying, the Cornish diocese was re-established at Truro. However, Truro wasn't the only candidate. Bodmin had been the medieval ecclesiastical centre of Cornwall, while the original Cornish See of St Germans also put forward a claim. There was even an enthusiastic vicar at St Columb who offered his church. The merits of each place were discussed and argued over. A Bill establishing the Diocese of Truro was finally passed by Parliament on 11 August 1876. The search for an architect and a design for a new cathedral could begin. The designs for many prestigious building projects have been chosen by submitting them to competition. For Truro Cathedral seven potential architects (GF Bodley, W. Burges, JL Pearson, RP Pullan, JP St Aubyn, JO Scott, and GE Street) were shortlisted to submit designs. To draw up completed designs for the project would have taken considerable time and the majority of the architects were against this method of selection and requested if they could submit drawings or photographs of previously designed buildings.

> " I push the heavy door open to a cathedral quiet and empty. The east window dances with colour in the morning sun. I feel the love and peace of the space as it draws me in and enfolds me. The chair I sit on, the pillar I touch, the arches that stretch away, turn my thoughts to those who laboured in faith to build it…and silently I give thanks. **Barbara, congregation member and volunteer**

In due course the Building Committee agreed to this course of action. The Executive Committee sat and deliberated, eventually casting seven votes for John Loughborough Pearson and four for George Bodley. On 20 August 1878 Pearson wrote and formally accepted the position as architect for Truro Cathedral:

> "I feel it is a great privilege to have to design and build such a work and I scarcely dared to hope that the chance of doing so would ever come to my lot…. I can only say that I will endeavour to do my best, with the means you may anticipate being able to lay out upon it."

The potential site of the new cathedral was challenging, to say the least. It occupied the lowest part of the town; it was sloping, hemmed in by shops and houses, and was the location of the old parish church of St Mary's. Because the church was in such a poor state of repair, Bishop Benson and the Building Committee wanted it to be demolished, but Pearson argued that it would cost as much to build a new chapel in the new building as it would to restore part of the old church, and so it was agreed to incorporate the south aisle of the church in the new cathedral, and to dedicate the whole building to the Blessed Virgin Mary.

1 Photograph c1887 showing completion of the first building phase.
2 Work in progress on the quire, October 1882. **3** The south aisle of the old St Mary's Parish Church was incorporated into the new Cathedral.

It was a very bold solution but it wasn't the only problem that the Building Committee had to overcome. There was no guarantee that enough money could be raised to complete the cathedral. An initial sum of £10,000 was spent acquiring the necessary land and preparing the site for the building, so that at least the laying of the foundation stone could go ahead. It was with much rejoicing and celebration that two foundation stones were laid on 20 May 1880 by the Duke of Cornwall (later Edward VII). As well as the traditional north-east corner foundation stone, another one was laid in the form of a granite pillar in what was then the churchyard of St Mary's. This base would eventually form one of the pillars in the nave of the Cathedral and was placed there as an act of faith that the building would eventually be completed. Great care was taken over the choice of granite stone for the walls of the building. Over 70 different types were investigated before granite from a Mabe quarry was chosen for the external walls, and stone from St Stephen for the interior. Bath stone was used internally and externally to provide the decorative detail for windows, statues and vaulting. Before any surface level work could be started, the underground crypt needed to be constructed. Once this was achieved it was agreed that the initial phase of the building scheme would include the completion of the east end, St Mary's aisle, the quire, the chancels and both transepts as far as the crossing. Seven years after the foundation stones were laid, the Cathedral was ready for use, and on 3 November 1887 the consecration service took place in the presence of the Archbishop of Canterbury, and former first Bishop of Truro, Dr EW Benson, who had helped lay the original foundation stone in 1880.

1 Laying of the 'Pillar of Faith' foundation stone, from a window in the Jesus Chapel. **2** Laying out the foundations for the nave.
3 View from high up in the west end looking down the nave.

There then began an extensive fundraising campaign that involved every parish and deanery in the county. It wasn't until 1899 that sufficient funds had been raised to allow the start of the construction of the nave. After four years of building the dedication of the nave took place on 15 July 1903. The Cathedral was at last taking shape; by 1905 the magnificent central Victoria Tower was completed, thanks to a £15,000 donation from James Hawke Dennis. The final piece of the jigsaw, the two western towers, was completed in 1910 after a donation from a Jane Ellen Hawkins. This brought to an end thirty years of uncertainty, and created the first new cathedral for generations; a testimony in stone for all those Cornish men and women whose faith and generosity had made the impossible become possible.

In 1880 John Loughborough Pearson was awarded the highly prestigious Royal Institute of British Architects (RIBA) Royal Gold Medal. The President of RIBA presented it "as a tribute not only of just admiration for the noble works of architecture which you have designed but also of sincere respect for your professional and private virtues". Pearson was at the height of his creative powers. He had recently been appointed as the architect for Truro Cathedral, a crowning moment of an illustrious career that spanned the entire period of the main Gothic Revival style. He was born on 5th July 1817, the thirteenth and last child of William Pearson, a water-colourist and engraver of Durham. At the age of fourteen he was articled to a Durham architect, Ignatius Bonomi, and for ten years strove to master the techniques of drawing plans, elevations, details and perspectives, as well as the more mundane activities of writing specifications and the surveying and laying out of sites. He also spent many hours sketching and drawing inside Durham Cathedral, something that was to stand him in good stead for the future. But Durham was hardly the cutting edge of architecture in the early part of the nineteenth century, and inevitably Pearson was drawn to London. In early 1842 he began working for Anthony Salvin, who was closely linked to the early Gothic Revival movement, and later Philip Hardwick, whom he helped with plans and drawings for the new hall and

1 Unusual view of the Cathedral taken with a fish-eye lens under the crossing. **2** One of JL Pearson's initial drawings of the proposed cathedral. **3** The ribbed vaulting in the baptistry is considered to be one of Pearson's great achievements.

2

3

library at Lincoln's Inn in Holborn. Pearson was also able to take on work on his own behalf, mainly in Yorkshire, where he built a number of country churches. However, his hopes of entering into a partnership with Hardwick came to nothing and he was forced to strike out on his own. As his reputation as an architect grew, Pearson began to travel extensively in Europe, visiting cathedrals in France (Amiens and Beauvais), Germany (Cologne, Aachen and Koblenz) and Belgium (Brussels and Liege). These and other visits clearly influenced Pearson and his design approach, marrying aspects of the Continental style with English traditions to create a synthesis of style that was all his own. St Peter's, Vauxhall was arguably Pearson's first great 'town church' – one that became the prototype of some of his best work in the 1870s and 1880s. St John's, Red Lion Square in Holborn;

St Augustine's, Kilburn; St Michael's, Croydon; and St John's, Upper Norwood are some of the finest churches built during the entire Gothic Revival period.

Pearson showed his creative genius in his ability to design three-dimensional spaces rather than in the conventional preoccupation with surface decoration. The plan always received his closest consideration and this helps to explain how Pearson managed to achieve a feeling of generous open space, even in the tightest of sites. His aim was first and foremost to create form, which he did by using proportion and contour and it is these qualities that speak most eloquently in his work.

John Loughborough Pearson was the only great Victorian architect whose career extended through the entire period of the Gothic Revival. He worked right up to his death in December 1897, when he was 80 years old. It was an appropriate tribute that, as befitting a leading architect of his generation, he was laid to rest in Westminster Abbey beside other eminent architects of the age, Barry, Scott and Street.

Pearson never saw his vision of the Cathedral realised, he died even before the nave had been completed. It fell to his son, Frank Pearson, to complete the task. Frank had already worked with his father for a number of years, and on his father's death he successfully took over the running of the family business.

"Does it send you to your knees?" This is the question you should ask, Pearson said, when you go into a church; not "Is this admirable? Is this beautiful?"

At Truro we definitely know the answer: get the kneelers out!

1 Statue of the architect holding his plan of the Cathedral.
2 Decorated stone arch and wooden finial. **Overleaf** the horizontal lines of the triforium are designed so that the eye is drawn to the risen Lord on the reredos behind the High Altar.

1

The Gothic Revival

The Gothic Revival was an architectural style that imitated the original medieval Gothic architecture, with its characteristic pointed arches. It developed during the eighteenth century but was at its height during the nineteenth, and to a certain extent replaced the Classical Revival style that had been popular before it. Two men were extremely influential in laying the foundations of what was to become the Gothic Revival. Augustus Pugin was a great admirer of medieval art and Gothic architecture. He wrote two of the basic texts of the Gothic Revival. In *Contrasts* (1836) he espoused the superiority of medieval life, and argued that Gothic architecture represented the perfect marriage of spiritual and artistic values. He developed his ideas in *The True Principles of Pointed or Christian Architecture* (1841), advocating that not only must Gothic detail be authentic but that the contemporary architect should achieve the structural clarity and high level of craftsmanship that were found in the Middle Ages by using the methods of medieval builders.

John Ruskin supplemented Pugin's ideas in his two hugely influential theoretical works, the *Seven Lamps of Architecture* (1849) and *The Stones of Venice* (1853). Finding his architectural ideal in Venice, Ruskin proposed that Gothic buildings excelled above all other architecture because of the moral truths expressed in their very fabric. He rejected the mechanisation and standardisation of the Industrial Revolution in favour of the stone-carvers' hand-crafted integrity.

This was also a time when the Church of England was undergoing a revival of its own. Influenced by the writings of the Oxford Movement, many believed that a more traditional Anglo-Catholic approach was the proper response to an increasing secularisation of society and decline in church attendance. There was also a need to build a large number of urban churches to cater for big shifts in population to the cities. The Gothic Revival style met those needs perfectly. The great secular buildings of this period include the magnificent Houses of Parliament designed by Pugin and Barry, and St Pancras Station in London, designed by Sir George Gilbert Scott.

Edward White Benson was born in 1829, the eldest of eight children, and attended King Edward's School in Birmingham. He seems to have had a natural leaning towards religion, even as a child creating his own chapel using a table covered in drapes as the altar, a home-made cross, and brass rubbings from a nearby church which he hung on the walls. Before he left school he was asked what he wanted to be. He replied "I should like to be a Canon, and recite the daily offices in my cathedral". In 1848 he went to Trinity College, Cambridge, where he read for a degree in classics and mathematics. At University he was secretary of the Cambridge Church Reading Society, organising meetings and delivering lectures. Notebooks surviving from his college days show his surprisingly detailed knowledge and interest of theology and liturgy. After leaving Cambridge Benson's first appointment was as a schoolmaster at Rugby School. As a boy he had been deeply impressed by the life of Dr Arnold, and so to be at the very school his hero had attended was a great ambition fulfilled. His duties were comparatively light and this enabled him to study for a fellowship at Cambridge, and to be ordained deacon in 1854 and priest in 1857. In 1859 Benson became the first headmaster of the newly founded Wellington College in Berkshire, which soon gained an excellent reputation for scholarship under his leadership. Benson helped plan the building of the new chapel and took great pride in designing the windows. The south transept of Truro Cathedral was a gift from the masters and scholars of Wellington in memory of their first headmaster.

In 1872 Benson was appointed Chancellor of Lincoln Cathedral, where his main duty was the training of theological students. He also organised and taught very successful Bible classes and night schools for the poor working class, and founded a temperance society. Although his tenure at Lincoln was relatively short it identified him as a true statesman of the Church and formed his view of the correct organisation of a cathedral. Lincoln came between his work at Wellington and Truro. At Lincoln the headmaster was gradually transformed into the bishop. On 25 April 1877 Edward White Benson was consecrated Bishop at St Paul's Cathedral. The following week, on 1 May, he was enthroned as the first Bishop of Truro in St Mary's Church and so began five hectic and remarkable years. Bishop Benson's achievements in Cornwall were astonishing. He restored the confidence of demoralised Anglican congregations amid the Methodist and Wesleyan fervour that had swept the county in the nineteenth century. He organised the establishment of a new diocese, the building of a new cathedral, the founding of a girls' high school, and won the respect and affection of the people of the county. Under Benson, church congregations increased, new churches and chapels of ease were consecrated and the clergy were encouraged to meet for discussion, mutual support and training. Lay associations provided a focus for licensed lay assistants, Sunday school teachers, readers, 'mission women' and class leaders. When in 1882 Benson was invited to become Archbishop of Canterbury, letters and tributes poured in from all over the county. There were brief notes from parishioners, formal letters from clergy, and a handsome bound volume containing signatures from every parish in the diocese, entitled 'Farewell Address from Cornwall'. The Bishop responded with his own 'Farewell to Cornwall' that showed a genuine sadness in leaving the county: "I have learnt to love every home and church and school".

His ability to work long hours and manage on very little sleep, his great energy and enthusiasm for new projects, his attention to detail, and his overriding concern for the people of his church were a reflection of his deep and vibrant faith and his Victorian belief that hard work brings you ever closer to God.

1 The Bishop Benson brass memorial in the south transept.
2 Bishop Benson's bust silhouetted against the south transept rose window. **3** Watercolour of the Cathedral's consecration in 1887.

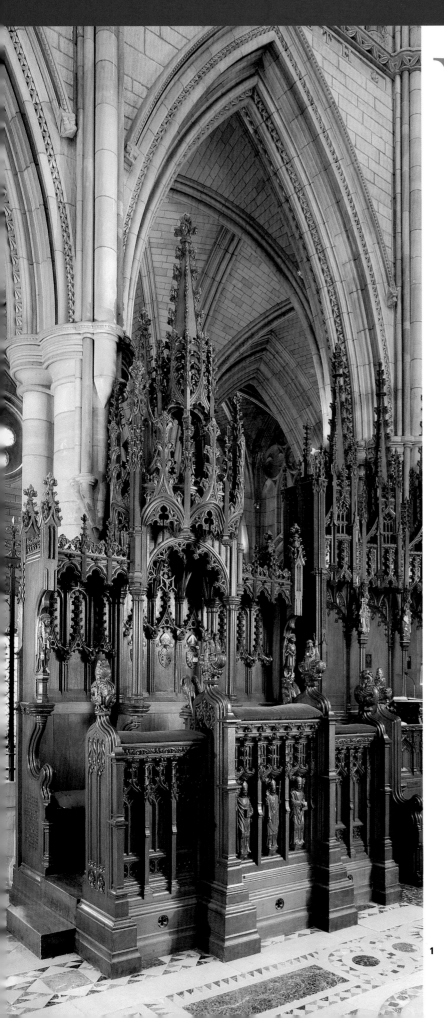

We pride ourselves on being Cornwall's Cathedral, and so we try to say 'yes' whenever we can to requests, for services and special events, concerts and exhibitions. A lot of our day-to-day activity is concerned with accommodating these requests and organising these events, and we are delighted to do it. But there is a downside to all this. We spend so much of our time responding to other people's agendas, that we have not always identified our own agenda as a Chapter and a Cathedral. It seems to us that we have a Gospel imperative to address this imbalance. Our thinking on these issues has been helped by a theological dictum of David Stancliffe, the Bishop of Salisbury, who says: "God in Christ comes to share our life and to transform it".

At the Cathedral, and perhaps this applies to other churches too, we have been rather better at emphasising the 'sharing' God than the 'transforming' God. We have agreed to every demand made of us because we believe that we can

1 2

meet the incarnate sharing God in all those we meet. Our story is God's story too, and we want to offer him our human creativity, aspirations and our fallibility. But the God who comes to share our life is also the God who meets us with unconditional love and unconditional demands, who issues us with a constant challenge to turn and to repent, both as individuals and as a society. He is often a counter-cultural God, a prophetic God, an uncomfortable God. As a Church that believes in this God who comes not only to share our life but also to transform it, we have a responsibility to work to transform the world, through the preaching of the Gospel of the cross, and its life-changing power for individuals and for society. This would mean a change from our largely reactive way of working, responding to the agendas of others, to a more proactive approach in which we seize the agenda for ourselves, as we seek to work out the challenges and glory of the Gospel for our life and our mission.

'Proactive' rather than 'reactive' – seizing the agenda for ourselves. This does not mean that we shall stop doing the things we have done in the past. We shall still want to say 'yes' whenever we can. But sometimes we shall need to say 'no', to allow us the time and space to do new things. These fall into four distinct categories.

1. Evangelism: Entering our wonderful building can be a converting experience in itself, and we hope that our carefully prepared and ordered worship with its glorious music will continue to lead many to God. But in future we want to be more overtly evangelistic, so that the promotion of Gospel teaching is at the heart of everything we do. We also plan to make more overt statements about our faith during the day, when most of our visitors are around: by using Gospel readings or appropriate prayers broadcast throughout the Cathedral; by using Scripture in our promotional material, including our revamped website and by providing more liturgical input in our new guidebooks.

2. Provocative and 'Political': We consider that the Cathedral is uniquely placed to raise difficult subjects and offer a platform to others whose voices might not otherwise be heard. We do this on behalf of the Bishop and the people of the diocese, sometimes by saying things that are more difficult for others to say.

3. Social issues: In the past, we have adopted a particular style and role that raises many questions about our mission. As one observer puts it: "You are very good at services, less good at service". We are keen to address this by putting Cathedral resources to the service of people and organisations that deal with social issues that affect the community at large.

4. Worship: We have become nationally recognised for the high standards of our choral tradition, gradually developing a worshipping style that is clearly Catholic, formal and dignified, yet unfussy, which has proved attractive and engaging to the majority of our regular worshippers. While not wanting to undermine any of that, we have questioned how our worship relates to those who are from a very different church tradition. If we are to be the Cathedral for everyone, how can we, for example, produce worship on special occasions that is more accessible and engaging to those from an Evangelical tradition, to young people, or to those from different social backgrounds from our own? We have made a start, through the excellent services featuring the music of Taizé, through the Rock Mass and Club JC for young people, and through Exalt Jesus where we have been working ecumenically. We will be looking for many more opportunities to offer a diversity of worship styles, as we ask God to work his transformation in our lives.

In these four ways we shall be seeking to pursue a more exciting and radical agenda in the next few years to try to become more and more a Cathedral that makes a difference to our county and our diocese.

3

1 The Bishop's Chair or Cathedra. **2** A staggering 100,000 prayer candles are lit each year in the Cathedral, by young and old alike. **3** Shoppers often pop into the Cathedral for a short rest and a quick prayer.

" Worship is at the heart of the Cathedral's life. At least three times a day we offer worship to God, and at least one of these services is a Eucharist or Communion Service when we break blessed bread and drink consecrated wine in remembrance of the death and resurrection of Jesus Christ. Christians believe that worshipping God – giving him thanks, saying sorry for our failures, asking him for his help and seeking his will – is the highest activity of which we are capable, and something which we do not only for ourselves and each other, but on behalf of the whole of creation.

1 The thurible is used in special services. It contains hot coals that burn incense producing billowing clouds of smoke, representing the prayers of people rising towards Heaven. **2** View of the St Mary's altar with the hanging pyx above. It contains the consecrated bread as an intense focus of the presence of Christ. **3** The chalice holds the consecrated wine during communion. **4** Receiving the consecrated wafer during communion.

My particular responsibility as Canon Precentor is to oversee all the arrangements for our worship. This includes the regular services, which often include music by our Cathedral Choir, as well as a large number of special services, which we organise to celebrate the great festivals of the Christian year, or for other significant occasions. Many local organisations work with us to plan these services, in which we try to express their hopes and concerns, as well as finding ways in which the Christian tradition reflects on these. The many detailed arrangements include asking: What sort of mood are we striving to create through this particular act of worship? What special music would be appropriate? Are there any dramatic features or symbolic actions which would add to the occasion? Are there special guests or representatives who need particular seats or who should be involved in leading the worship? How is the event to be publicised? To whom should the proceeds of the collection be donated? As well as choosing material from the Bible and existing prayer books, often new material will need to be specially written, and sometimes research is necessary into the background of an organisation so that the liturgy strikes just the right note. And then there is a whole army of people within the Cathedral organisation who need to be informed and consulted about the service.

The Cathedral lends itself to worship in a fairly formal style, and the majority of our regular services fall into that pattern. But that is not the whole story. We also aim to provide special services in a whole variety of styles: meditative services by candlelight using the music of Taizé; services designed with young people especially in mind; evangelistic services; acts of worship which are designed to be provocative and challenging; ecumenical services in the styles of other Christian traditions; and special occasions where Christians pray alongside those of other faiths.

Meanwhile the daily round of worship continues. Sometimes it attracts a large congregation; sometimes just a few people join the choir and the clergy for a midweek Evensong. But we aim to approach each act of worship with the same attention to detail, for we believe that the offering to God of our best powers of mind and heart is at the centre of our Cathedral life. 〞

Canon Perran Gay, Precentor

2   3

1 A mirror in the organ loft allows the organist to keep an eye on the congregation.
2 High Altar Cross designed by JL Pearson. **3** The candle bearers (acolytes) wait to process into a cathedral service.

1

It is said that few sounds on earth are more glorious than an English Cathedral choir in full voice; that they are the lifeblood, the animating factor that turns a cathedral from a beautiful but silent space into one that reverberates with glory. Truro Cathedral Choir has one of the best musical reputations in the country, singing six choral services each week in term time. The music is carefully integrated with the magnificent liturgy of the Cathedral and is exceptionally wide-ranging. The repertoire encompasses some of the greatest music from the fourteenth century to the present day. This great tradition continues with the Cathedral commissioning new works from celebrated composers such as Paul Comeau, David Briggs, Gabriel Jackson and Russell Pascoe. Beyond its regular worship duties the choir of eighteen boys and twelve men also perform at least three concerts a year, record critically acclaimed CDs and feature regularly on radio and television, they sometimes even find time to go on tour! It takes a lot of commitment and energy to be a member of the choir! The Cathedral itself supports the musical education of the young choristers by providing bursaries and other choral scholarships for a number of students each year. This continued support is absolutely vital to delivering consistently high musical standards to which the Cathedral Choir aspires.

4

"For me the music at Truro Cathedral is second to none. It never fails to raise my spirits no matter how I'm feeling. Whether through the subtlety of a gentle introit, or the power of a resounding voluntary, the music enhances the spiritual occasion. At its best, music has the power to lift the soul, and I think that's true whether one has a strong personal faith or none at all. **Martin, a music lover**

1 **2**

3

1 The Cathedral Choir in full voice at one of their concerts. **2** The choir consists of eighteen boys and twelve men singing six choral services a week in term time. **3** A few of the choristers in relaxed mode. **4** An attentive chorister.

The highlight of the Choir year for many people is the Festival of Nine Lessons and Carols, made famous by King's College Choir, Cambridge on radio and television. This service actually originated here in Truro when Edward White Benson, the first Bishop of Truro, put together the service for Christmas Eve in 1880. Nowadays the Christmas Eve Service attracts a congregation of well over a thousand people, and in recent years Chapter has been delighted to hold a second 'Nine Lessons' on 23 December so that no one is ever turned away.

Recently a membership scheme, Truro Cathedral Music, has been started which is designed to help support the living musical tradition at the Cathedral. If you would like to know more about the scheme or for any other musical enquiry please contact the Director of Music at the Cathedral Office (for details see the contents page).

Truro Cathedral has the most extensive organ recital series of any cathedral in the country with over 30 recitals from March to October. We attract recitalists from all over the world and our audiences are bowled over by the sound and quality of the famous Father Willis organ. How has this musical instrument generated such interest and affection? It was installed in the Cathedral in 1887 and remains uniquely in its original tonal state – one of the masterpieces of nineteenth-century musical instrument making. The organ was built in London and transported to Cornwall by boat! In terms of its specification, the organ reveals standard Willis hallmarks – tierce mixtures on Great and Swell, characterful gedackts on the Choir, and a small but telling pedal division. There is no doubt that Willis was one of the greatest organ builders there has ever been. At Truro we see the quintessence of his art as a voicer. The fine position of the instrument in its own fan-vaulted chamber certainly adds to its impact and matches the resonant cathedral acoustic perfectly.

1 The music library contains work from the Middle Ages to the present day. **2** The pipes of the Father Willis organ occupy the first two bays of the quire on the north side. **3** Nimble footwork on the organ pedals. **4** The organ stops are controls that help to produce different sounds on the organ.

"Greetings from Victoria, British Columbia, Canada, where I'm sitting at my computer listening 'live' to your broadcast of Choral Evensong. I just want to pass on my congratulations to Robert Sharpe and Christopher Gray, and the choir of Truro Cathedral on a spectacular Evensong. "
BBC Radio 3 listener

1

2

3

One should remember that the nave of the Cathedral was not constructed until the first decade of the 20th century, so Willis voiced the organ for a building that did not yet actually exist in its entirety – surely a mark of genius! Willis built an organ of superb reliability. Apart from the addition of the electric blower in the 1920s, no major work was done until 1963, when the grandson of the original builder carried out a conservative restoration together with a relocation of the console over on to the south side in a new gallery placed above the choir stalls. Here the organist can not only hear the instrument in its full glory, but also maintain close contact with the Cathedral Choir. In 1991 the organ was again fully restored, this time by the organ builders N P Mander Ltd of London.

Each year the Cathedral supports an organ scholar, usually one in their gap year, to further their musical education. They help with the organ-playing duties and take a full part in the life of the Cathedral.

'Simply one of the best musical instruments in the world.' This seems to be a rather grandiose claim, until you see what some of the best organists in the world say about the Cathedral's organ:

4

"A truly fabulous beast!! "
Wayne Marshall

"At last I got to play this wonderful organ. " **David Sanger**

"The organ seems even finer than my first encounter with it. Superb! " **Simon Preston**

1

1 *Cornubia, Land of the Saints,* painted by John Miller and unveiled in the Cathedral's centenary year, 1980, by HRH Prince Charles.

There is one particular painting in the Cathedral that is invariably surrounded by visitors. It seems to attract and hold their attention in a very special way. The painting is a bird's eye view of Cornwall looking westwards towards the Isles of Scilly and the Atlantic. Painted over the landscape are tiny crosses marking the position of parish churches; many of them dedicated to Celtic Saints with strange sounding names such as Cuby, Issey, Petroc, Ruan, Uny and Winwaloe. These names are not only remembered in these church dedications but also appear in profusion in the place names of villages and towns of Cornwall. Floating above the land, the artist has painted an army of Saints arriving from the west bringing the light of the Gospel and the Holy Spirit to Cornwall. This is Cornwall, Land of the Saints.

" There are more Saints in Cornwall than there are in heaven. "
Old Cornish saying

To find the origin of these place names we need to look back to the last throes of Rome's Christian Empire. By 410AD Rome had withdrawn its legions from Britain, effectively leaving her defenceless. The gradual invasion and settlement by pagan Germanic tribes in the east of England was met with limited resistance. The light of Christ was extinguished here until the mission of St Augustine to Kent, to convert the Saxons in AD597. The fall of the Roman Empire was a rather chaotic and patchy affair; in some areas life carried on much as normal while in others all traces of occupation were wiped out. What is clear is that many of the Christian communities, especially in Wales and the South West, continued and thrived as centres of education, learning and mission. It was in this period from the fifth to the seventh centuries that young men and women, many trained in the great Welsh monasteries, embraced the life of missionary preachers filled with the fire and passion of the Holy Spirit and kept the light of Christianity alive. They would leave their homes and travel across the seas, establishing small oratories or churches as they went. Sustained by their great love and ardour for the Gospel, their sole possessions would be a staff and a hand bell. Some of these Peregrini or 'wandering saints' may have ended up as martyrs, but whatever their particular fate, all of them left their mark on the land of Cornwall. Some of their journeys can be traced by looking at the church dedications and place names as they criss-crossed the seaways and countries of the Atlantic seaboard (Ireland, Wales, Cornwall and Brittany).

4

2 **3**

2 Reredos from the Jesus Chapel altar painted by Annie Walke, one of the Newlyn School of painters. It shows Christ blessing Cornish industry as it was in the 1930s.
3 St Piran's flag is also the flag of Cornwall. 4 Carved wooden statue of St Piran in the quire carrying his staff and a model of his oratory, now buried in the sands at Perranporth.

St Piran and St Petroc are perhaps the most revered Celtic Saints in Cornwall. St Piran is remembered in place names like Perranporth, Perranuthnoe and Perran ar worthal, echoing his name down through the centuries. St Petroc has at least six churches dedicated in his memory. St Piran's feast day is 5 March and is celebrated in Cornwall by walks and marches to special places associated with him, such as his buried oratory near Perranporth. The Cathedral is given over to dancing and singing school children and is full of their artwork and colourful displays. The St Piran flag is the flag of Cornwall; it has a white cross on a black background and can be seen proudly flying from many flagpoles and buildings in the county. It is said to represent the light of Christ being brought into the dark of the world.

In Cornwall the sound of bells calling people to worship can be traced back to the Age of Saints (5th–7th century AD). As the Celtic Saints travelled around the countryside they would ring hand bells to gather people for worship and to listen to their preaching. Saint Petroc's bell was kept at Bodmin for many years and was revered to the extent that legal agreements were sworn with one hand on the bell, in the same manner as touching a Bible or a crucifix. At least two of these types of hand bell are preserved in Brittany, one at St Pol de Leon and one at St Meryadoc. It is thus very fitting that the Cathedral bells, all bar one, should be named after various Cornish and Celtic Saints.

The main set of ten bells in the Cathedral is housed in the NW tower of the west front. The bells are rung to call people to worship for half an hour before the main services on Sunday and to mark special national and diocesan occasions. This ringing peal was hung in two tiers by John Taylor & Co. of Loughborough and was first rung at their dedication service on 21 June 1910. The sound of the bells was so loud that the girls operating the switchboard at the local telephone exchange in High Cross couldn't hear their callers! The remedy was to try to muffle the sound of the bells using soundproofing mattresses that effectively mellowed the sound of the bells in the immediate vicinity. The ringing chamber is excellently positioned in its own gallery beneath the bells and also contains the Library of the Diocesan Guild of Ringers.

3

4

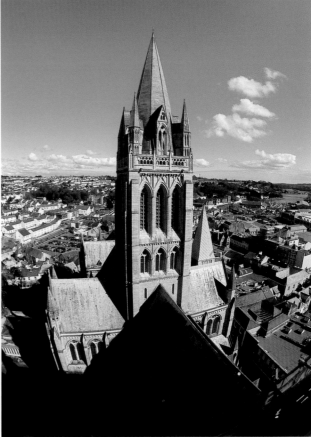

1 **2**

1 A view from the floor of the ringing chamber. **2** The bells in the upright position, ready for ringing. **3** St Piran with his hand bell from the north transept window. **4** View of central tower, and Truro, from the bell tower.

THE BELLS OF TRURO CATHEDRAL

Bell	Name of bell	Cwts	Qtr	Lbs
Treble	St Mary & Nicholas	6	I	19
2	St Kea	6	3	17
3	St Piran	7	2	17
4	St Petroc	7	3	26
5	St Germans	8	3	9
6	St Nectan	10	3	16
7	St Agnes	14	I	12
8	St Kenwyn	18	I	18
9	St Madron & St Gulval	23	3	4
Tenor	St Probus & St Grace	33	3	10

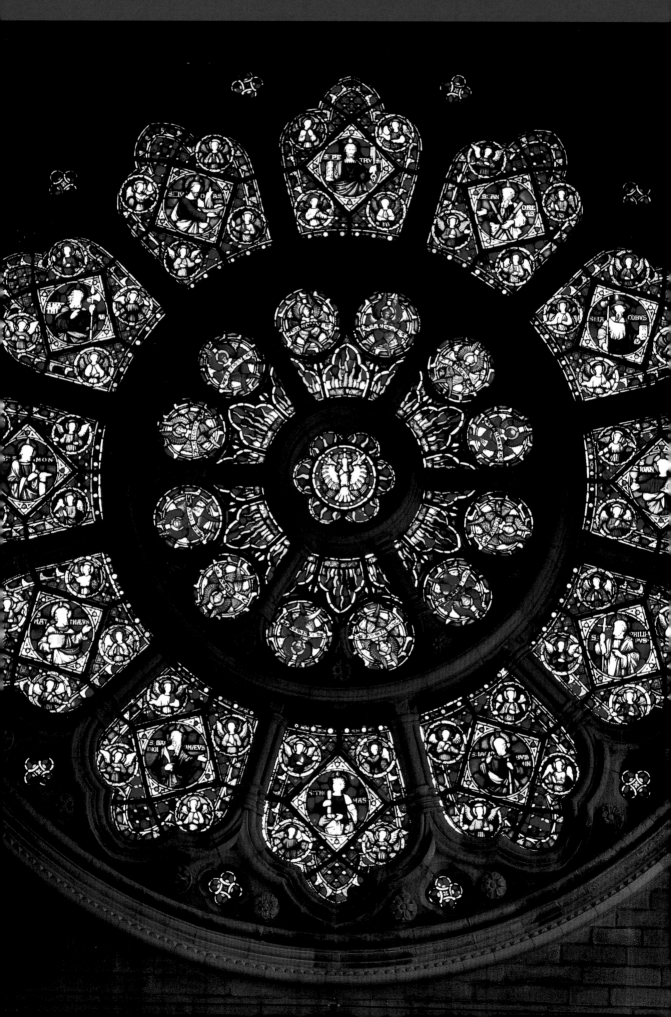

> Then God said, 'Let there be light'; and there was light. And God saw that the light was good; and God separated the light from the darkness. God called the light Day, and the darkness he called Night.
>
> **Genesis: Chapter 1 (v.3–5)**

The art of stained glass-making has been practised in England for nearly 1,400 years, with the earliest recorded glass, probably in the form of a mosaic, being at Monkwearmouth monastery (Sunderland) in 675AD. The origins of church stained glass are obscure but it is thought that it began in the Byzantine world, gradually spreading to the rest of Europe. What is more certain is that the stained glass industry was well established in England by the early twelfth century, when the complex techniques of stained glass manufacture had been developed. These techniques took a further leap forward when the Gothic architectural style gained prominence in the thirteenth-century. Its thinner walls and bigger window spaces meant more scope for developing and introducing ever bigger and more colourful schemes. Unfortunately a lot of the original medieval glass in churches and cathedrals in Britain has been destroyed, either during the Reformation or later during the Commonwealth, so that twelfth and thirteenth century glass is now very rare. The stained glass destruction also meant a gradual loss and decline of the skills and techniques required to make and repair it. In fact it wasn't until the early decades of the nineteenth century and the Victorian Gothic Revival that these lost skills and techniques were rediscovered in this country, leading to a massive renaissance of stained glass manufacture.

The process of making stained glass has remained largely unaltered through the centuries and involves the manufacture of coloured glass, known as 'pot-metal'. This is made by adding various metallic oxides to the crucibles in which the glass is melted. Iron oxide gives a red colouring, copper oxide green and cobalt blue. The molten glass is then blown and shaped into sheets of 'antique' glass. Because some of these were found to be too opaque to produce the lightness and luminosity required, a technique of 'flashing' a thin layer of the coloured glass onto ordinary glass was developed. True 'stained glass' is made by painting the outside surface with silver nitrate, which after firing in the kiln produces yellow and gold colours. The detailed design for the window is drawn at full scale with the different sections of coloured

Rose Window

complex, folded in on herself
rose holds the dove
radiates from her rose-self
a floribundance of flame
bursting into flickering tongues
orange, red then redness aflame
with orange again and again
and around them flower
twelve angels in blue and red
red and blue, fly and spiral
from the wheel's whirl of rose
rise from the dove's wings –
the enclosed garden grows
flowers into apostles
set in the squares of their circles
while this rational rose
petalled and curved
spinning wheels of creation
fast cycles of earth, red days
of moon and slow rhythms of sun
holds twelve holy men spun
from her rose-centre
set alight by wings of cool white
forever aflame, aflame, aflame

**Victoria Field, Writer in Residence
(2005–2006)**

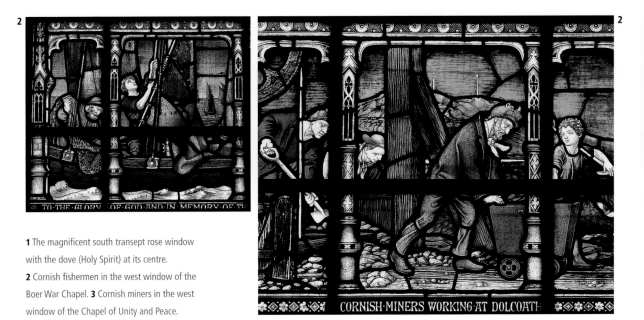

1 The magnificent south transept rose window with the dove (Holy Spirit) at its centre.
2 Cornish fishermen in the west window of the Boer War Chapel. **3** Cornish miners in the west window of the Chapel of Unity and Peace.

CORNISH·MINERS·WORKING·AT·DOLCOATH

glass identified. These are then cut to the right shape. Next, figures and shading are painted onto the glass using a black pigment. A small kiln is then used to fuse one to the other. These panes are laid over the drawn design and joined to each other using lead strips. Finally the panels of glass are held in place by metal bars set in the surrounding stonework and by copper wire tied and soldered to them. A medieval craftsman would easily recognise this technique. In our age of global communication, when computers can send and receive emails around the world in fractions of a second it is difficult to conceive of a time when communication consisted almost entirely of word of mouth in an essentially illiterate world. It is in that earlier context that stained glass provided a key communication tool to teach Christian faith and beliefs. Subject matter would therefore include scenes from the Old and New Testaments, the genealogy of Christ (especially popular) and the lives and miracles of the Saints.

1 The Wesley window, John standing, Charles seated on the left. The lower image is John Wesley preaching at Gwennap Pit. **2** God the Father at the heart of the Creation rose window: 'Fiat Lux', let there be light. **3** Angel from the Creation rose window, showing the incredible level of detail in the windows. **4** Window light commemorating the laying of the foundation stone in 1880, and window celebrating the life of Queen Victoria.

EDWARD · FIRST · BISHOP · OF · TRURO

FOUNDATION · OF · TRURO · CATHEDRAL

· GORDO· · QUEEN · VICTORIA · · ENNYSON ·

·QUEEN·VICTORIA·RECEIVING·THE·NEWS·OF·HER·ACCESSION·

The world's largest stained glass project!

The glass at Truro Cathedral is the largest stained glass project ever made. It is also some of the finest Victorian stained glass to be found anywhere in the world. The whole integrated scheme was designed by Bishop Benson and the architect, JL Pearson, and was manufactured by the London firm of Clayton & Bell. Unfortunately, most of the original drawings and plans were destroyed in the 1940 Blitz, although the Cathedral does have a watercolour sketch for the proposed stained glass in the north-east transept windows (not completed). Benson and Pearson's scheme was for 85 individual lights and three rose windows.

1 & 2 Scenes from the life of Henry Martyn from the windows in the baptistry. **3** The Last Supper from the lower lights in the east window. **4** The magnificent upper east window, celebrating Christ's victory over death.

" My favourite place in the Cathedral is the transept crossing, the hub of the building's cruciform shape and the only place where all three rose windows can be seen. The rose windows portray the Holy Trinity, the basis of Christian faith. These masterpieces of the glazier's art are set in Pearson's tracery designs, each of which is subtly different. Turning away from the roses to the east window, we have the complex splendour of Christ in Majesty, giving a spiritual dimension of light and colour to the Quire. What a fitting climax to all the narratives embodied in the sequence of windows; what skill, what imagination, what vision! " **Michael, congregation member and volunteer**

1   2   3   4

All the windows were donated by benefactors and so were completed as and when donors came forward. The last window was inserted in 1938. The one area where the scheme is still incomplete is the clerestory, the highest windows in the Cathedral. Here mostly plain glass has been used as few people wanted window dedications at a height where they couldn't be seen! The overall stained glass scheme has several different narratives running through it, each developed in a different part of the Cathedral. The story is essentially of God's ongoing relationship with humanity, from the Creation, through the Old and New Testaments and throughout history up to the point at which the foundation stone was laid. So the three rose windows represent the Holy Trinity, the clerestories were to depict the Old Testament sequence; the Gospel story is illustrated in the quire, while the windows on the main floor show the unfolding story of Christianity in England. They demonstrate the work of the Holy Spirit in the lives of saints, scholars, kings, queens, bishops, martyrs, artists, musicians and poets.

This large terracotta frieze is the work of George Tinworth and is probably the most admired piece of sculpture in the Cathedral. The two things that strike you about it are the level of detail and the composition. The inspiration for the composition is taken from the gospel of St Luke as Christ carries the cross to the site of his Crucifixion. George Tinworth rose from extreme poverty to become one of the foremost sculptors of his day, working for Doultons at Lambeth, to produce both commercial 'art pottery' and public commissions for churches, buildings and parks. Doultons used him as a figurehead sculptor to promote the work of the company at international exhibitions. This sculpture was given to the Cathedral in 1902 by Mr FW Bond in thanks for the safe return of his two sons from the South African War.

1 Christ addressing the daughters of Jerusalem. **2** Crowd trouble. **3** Barabbas shielding his eyes, having just been released from prison. **4** Simon of Cyrene being made to help carry the cross. **5** Full view of the terracotta.

4

" Pilate released the man they asked for (Barabbas), the one who had been put in prison for insurrection and murder, and he handed Jesus over as they wished. As they led him away, they seized a man, Simon of Cyrene, who was coming from the country, and they laid the cross on him, and made him carry it behind Jesus. A great number of the people followed him, and among them were women who were beating their breasts and wailing for him. But Jesus turned to them and said, 'Daughters of Jerusalem, do not weep for me, but weep for yourselves and for your children. For the days are surely coming when they will say, "Blessed are the barren, and the wombs that never bore, and the breasts that never nursed" '. "

Luke: Chapter 23 (v.25–29)

5

CALVARY

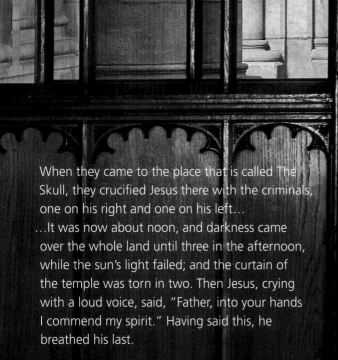

When they came to the place that is called The
Skull, they crucified Jesus there with the criminals,
one on his right and one on his left…
…It was now about noon, and darkness came
over the whole land until three in the afternoon,
while the sun's light failed; and the curtain of
the temple was torn in two. Then Jesus, crying
with a loud voice, said, "Father, into your hands
I commend my spirit." Having said this, he
breathed his last.

Luke: Chapter 23 (v.33, 44–46)

JOSEPH WELLINGTON
HUNKIN
1935 – BISHOP – 1950

JOHN MAURICE KEY
BISHOP OF TRURO
1960   1973

The Jerusalem Trust presented
this set of four paintings
by Craigie Aitchison to the
Chapter of Truro Cathedral
on 19 June 1997.

1

"The Craigie Aitchison *Calvary* has made St Margaret's Chapel a special place for me and one to which I am always glad to return. When the panels were installed it was suggested that we should take time, to simply sit and respond to them, without rushing to make artistic judgements or intellectual statements.

For me, the scene has been pared down '…they crucified Jesus there with the criminals, one on his right, and one on his left.' Like the icons of Orthodox Christianity, the stylised forms in the painting give me deeper insights into the significance of this event than detailed and graphic descriptions of the physical suffering of Christ. Like the Gospel writers, Craigie Aitchison's intention appears to be to let the event speak for itself and not to superimpose his own interpretation. I don't think it is sentimental to look to the Bedlington terrier, gazing up in contemplation at the youthful figure of the crucified Christ, for an example of how to approach the painting and the mystery and meaning of the Crucifixion.

I see Jesus, as so often in the Gospels, in the company of the marginalised and the outcast, and sharing their fate. However, the sense of desolation created by the starkness of the scene and the pastry-like lifeless arms of the thieves, is transformed by the shaft of light from Heaven. It suggests that Christ is the beloved Son who fulfils the will of the Father and reigns from the cross in glory. I wonder about the ram-like animal in the third panel – does it recall the ram caught in the thicket that took the place of Isaac in Abraham's sacrifice? Here there is a reversal of that story, Jesus the Son offers himself – the Lamb of God indeed.

The presence of the animals and bird helps me to appreciate the cosmic significance of the Crucifixion and I rejoice that the beautiful hills in the background are already lit with a subtle golden light. The fourth panel reinforces this sense of optimism with the twig, full of hope, pointing beyond the painting – out you go and live the insights you have gained from your contemplation of the great mystery of the Crucifixion!

Perhaps on my next visit I shall leave with different reflections."

Charles, congregation member and volunteer

1 The four *Calvary* images.
2 The High Altar with the reredos screen behind.

2

The focus of any church or cathedral is the High Altar. Communion, the sharing of bread and wine representing Christ's great sacrifice of body and blood, is at the heart of Christian worship. The High Altar is the table upon which the bread and wine are prepared before distribution to the congregation. The origins of Communion are simply and clearly outlined in the following lines from the gospel of St Matthew:

"While they were eating, Jesus took a loaf of bread, and after blessing it he broke it, gave it to the disciples, and said, 'Take, eat; this is my body.' Then he took a cup, and after giving thanks he gave it to them, saying, 'Drink from it, all of you; for this is my blood of the covenant, which is poured out for many for the forgiveness of sins.'" Matthew: Chapter 26 (v.26–28)

Behind the High Altar the magnificent carved reredos by Nathaniel Hitch provides an incredible backdrop. It is a wonderfully decorated screen, made from Bath stone, and showing various Biblical scenes that echo Christ's great sacrifice. There was supposed to be a further part to the top of the screen, but this was never completed due to lack of funds.

1

2

1 The Tree of Life, symbol of the sacrament of Life in paradise.
2 Christ seated in Majesty, hand raised in blessing.
3 The Shew Bread, symbol of the consecration of the twelve tribes of Israel. **4** Christ crucified.

3

“The great reredos in Truro Cathedral is a 'magical work' in which its creator, Nathaniel Hitch, has made stone do what normally by its nature it cannot do, and that is speak two messages at once. The central and powerful panels of the reredos show Christ seated in glory above a Christ suffering in agony on the cross. The magic comes when simply gazing at the piece. Whichever element you have in focus you cannot escape 'seeing' the other in your peripheral vision. It is as if the stone is 'saying' that when you look at the Christ figure seated in glory it is the same as looking at him in agony. ”
Canon Paul (Treasurer 1994–2003)

It is very fitting that the first piece of church furniture given to the Cathedral should be the place from where the Bible is read each week. It was given to the Cathedral by Miss Henrietta Lanyon in 1877, the year the Diocese of Truro was formed, and stood for a while in the old parish church before work on the new cathedral had even begun. Eagle lecterns are commonly found in churches and are full of symbolism. In classical mythology the eagle was able to look into the sun and even fly into it, burning away the deposit of age and renewing its youth. Thus it was used in early Christian times as a symbol of Christ's resurrection and that of the righteous Christian. It was also used as a symbol for St John the Evangelist because his Gospel sees most clearly into the light and divinity of Christ, as the eagle was able to gaze into the sun. Standing on a golden globe the eagle has vanquished the serpent (the devil), symbolising its ultimate triumph over evil. The globe beneath the eagle represents the world from which he is rising, as he gazes at the divine nature of Christ. It also represents the world to which the Gospel is to be preached, for the Gospel, like the church whose task it is to proclaim it, is turned in two directions, toward Christ and toward the world that Christ has redeemed.

2

1 "The light shines in the darkness, and the darkness did not overcome it". **2** Reading the Word of God.

"Establishing communication with others is relatively easy when you are sprawled inelegantly on the nave floor with Brasso and duster in hand. 'How long does it take?' or, 'My wife used to clean the brass at our church, but she's dead now', or 'I polished my war medals with Brasso'. The ice is broken, the first words spoken – the hardest part for people to lead into sharing something of themselves is overcome. Thank God for the lectern, the Brasso and the elbow grease and for the connections made. How long does it take? Well, the answer is, like the Forth Bridge, when you think you've finished it's time to start again. "
Hilary, lectern cleaner (1980–2004)

All buildings require maintenance and repair, but here in Truro we have a particularly difficult problem. The Bath stone (Stoke Grand Base Bed) used at high levels for decorative carved work has not weathered well and is disintegrating. JL Pearson, the architect, worked a great deal with Bath stone on many different projects and indeed he originally conceived of the entire Cathedral being built of it. However, in the Cornish climate the stone has failed and we are having to replace the defective stonework around the exterior of the Cathedral. Because all the work is at high levels it is a very expensive process. A research project carried out at Hallam University in Sheffield and funded by English Heritage sought to identify a similar-looking but much more hardwearing stone. The results were carefully analysed by a panel of experts, and a Cotswold stone, Syerford, was identified as the most suitable alternative stone. A fifteen-year programme has begun to replace the failing Bath stone with Syerford stone. In 2002 the east end was restored. In 2005 the Cathedral celebrated the 125th anniversary of the laying of the foundation stones. It also saw a £730,000 restoration of the west front. By 2012 and the 125th anniversary of the consecration, or first use of the Cathedral, we hope to have completed the restoration of the 250ft central Victoria Tower.

3

2

1 One of the twenty stonemasons at work on the recent west front restoration. **2** Careful cleaning and inspection within the Cathedral. **3** Restoration work on the north-west tower. **Overleaf** The fully restored west front in all its glory.

These are necessary works but not our main task. Inspiration will be at the heart of all that we shall be seeking to achieve in the next few years. We are entering a time of great excitement and anticipation, tempered with recognition of the daunting task ahead, "as we try to become more and more a Cathedral that makes a difference to our county and our diocese".